Open
Your
Hearts

Open
Your
Hearts

Huub Oosterhuis

TRANSLATED BY DAVID SMITH

HERDER AND HERDER

1971
HERDER AND HERDER NEW YORK
232 Madison Avenue, New York 10016

Original edition: *In het voorbijgaan* (second half),
© 1968, Uitgeverij Ambo, Utrecht, The Netherlands.

Library of Congress Catalog Card Number: 74–140237
© 1971 by Herder and Herder, Inc.
Manufactured in the United States

Contents

The Breaking of the Bread

In our churches and chapels there is a stone table, immovable, monumental, and usually very valuable. Instead of this, there should perhaps be a wooden table, sober and distinct. And on this wooden table there should be—instead of gold ciboria—wooden plates or woven baskets. And in them bread like the bread that we have on our tables at home.

Standing around that table, we do various things with that bread. It is broken and shared, given away. People come forward and receive the bread in their open hands and say "amen" or nowadays simply "thank you."

A few simple gestures, no sleight-of-hand. What do we aim to express in this rite, this game? Perhaps we want to demonstrate our consent to the gospel that has been announced to us, by presenting a sign, joining in, believing with our hands. If a person is not ready to give this sort of answer or if he does not want want to commit himself to what he has heard, he can of course just remain seated.

It is, then, a gesture of consent and of our belonging together: we all receive a piece of the same bread. The gesture of breaking bread, something that has been handed down to us from the earliest Church, is as deep and

1

meaningful and extends as far as our sense of belonging together.

People belong together in countless ways and they share this world, this life with each other in countless variations. On a small piece of land there is a great block of flats, in each of which you can hear everything that is going on next door, above, and below. Along a little part of a street there are thousands of people, hurrying, nervous people all trying to overtake each other. We share whatever space there is, whatever prosperity, words or happiness—double happiness. And sorrow—half sorrow. Or double sorrow. What was it? We share everything that it is possible to share and we are given our share of war and peace, usually without asking.

When are you a person? If you share other people's lives, if you are given a part to play in the happiness of another person. If you can give and receive, if you are taken, accepted. There is a poem by Jan Elburg about what "life" is. It is, he says,

being eaten
to be a man, to be a woman,
above all to be a person once again
and to gather oneself in love.

In some way or another, intuitively, by experience, every person knows that giving and sharing has everything to do with happiness. That you have to break and to give away and that, unless you do this, you are not living. Who would we be, what would we be, if that had not been done to us, if we had not received, if we had not been received? We would have been souls stifled, not at birth, but in embryo—certainly not people. You are fed until you become someone who can feed others—"somebody," one person among many, the average man.

He is called Adam in the Bible. The columnist Simon Carmiggelt calls him a little man like all of us. The average man marries, has a little piece of the world (a given situation), children, friends. He works—happily, with ambition, reluctantly, because he has to, because he wants to. He works with his head and his hands and his soul, and his work is worth something. It is worth money and it is answered by money. The average man turns himself into money, earning for himself and for the other people who have been given to him, supporting them, providing bread, housing, freedom, holidays. You could almost say: in the bread that is on the table at home, he himself is on the table, he himself becomes that bread, food for his children. "This is me," he might almost say, when he breaks and shares the bread, "this is my body." And everyone would understand what he meant:

being eaten
to be a man, to be a woman,
above all to be a person once again
and to gather oneself in love.

It is only when you yourself have become "someone" that you begin to understand what you have for a long time past experienced personally: that you live by the grace of . . . yes, of what? the sacrifice of others? Perhaps that word is too heavy, too dramatic. That you live by the grace and the work and the faithfulness of others. It is faithfulness that perpetuates this event of a man who becomes money, bread, life for others, a man for others, and makes it last. He finds his happiness in this faithfulness—and his death. For every day of work is a piece of himself, every year of work is a year of his body. Living, then, is being used up, becoming antiquated and worn out, slowly but surely dying. He is sown like seed in that piece of the world that is assigned to him, he is reaped like corn, threshed and beaten, ground and gathered to make bread, he is eaten to be a person once again. That is the way it is. It goes almost without saying. Every farmer knows that. The grain of wheat that dies is the image and likeness of man, though not a tragic image. There is no cosmic disaster, no sun falling from the sky, but something too small to be seen, a very ordinary event, something that almost happens between the paving stones in the street. There is no visible pain, and if it happens to you and you are that man who is a grain of wheat, then you think it is better that way.

In the gospel, the grain of wheat is the image and likeness of Jesus of Nazareth, the son of men who did not live for himself and did not die for himself. The gospel calls him bread for the life of the world and knows that he expressed the mystery of his life in a meaningful gesture, that he broke the bread and gave it to be eaten and thus to be the new man. The Church, which must be born again and again from the gospel, recognizes in that gesture of Jesus of Nazareth the mystery of life itself, for no one lives for himself and no one dies for himself.

Breaking bread and sharing it with each other, holding out your open hand: these little, defenseless gestures, always the same, are gestures towards him. And they might mean that we want to remember him, keep him in mind, imitate him in our lives, go out to meet him in hope, that we see salvation in the man he was and in the God he called his Father, that we believe in giving and receiving, in belonging together, in the mystery of our own lives.

It is also rather a desperate gesture, in which we admit that we cannot quite complete it and that we do not know how it has to be done on a world-wide scale, breaking bread and sharing it. It is an impotent gesture against world hunger, an expression of collective guilt. We use an image and sense that it is still not a reality. But at the same time we also admit in this gesture that we hold to that vision of a future world where there is justice, where we do not tear each other to pieces, but do what is unthinkable and impossible and are what we cannot be yet—people living in peace.

Ten Table Prayers

Also called "canons of the mass"
or "great prayers of thanksgiving."

To be used
in the celebration of the Eucharist
before the breaking and sharing
of the bread.

To keep alive the memory
of Jesus of Nazareth.

The name of God blessed and spoken,
his words and deeds
clearly demonstrated,
the "death of the Lord" proclaimed.

A kind of psalm.

1.

The Lord will be with you.
   The Lord will preserve you.
Lift up your hearts.
   Our hearts are with the Lord.
Let us thank the Lord our God.
   He is worthy of our gratitude.

We thank you
for you are a God of people,
for we may call you our God and Our Father,
for you hold our future in your hands,
for this world touches your heart.

You called us and broke through our deafness,
you appeared in our darkness,
you opened our eyes with your light,
you ordered everything for the best for us
and brought us to life.

Blessed are you, the source of all that exists.
We thirst for you,
because you have made us thirsty.
Our hearts are restless
until we are secure in you,
with Jesus Christ our Lord.

With all who have gone before us in faith,
we praise your name, O Lord our God.
You are our hope
and we thank you, full of joy,
adoring you with the words:

Holy, holy, holy,
Lord of all powers.
Heaven and earth
are full of your glory.
Come and deliver us,
Lord most high.
Blessed is he who comes
in the name of the Lord.

Come and deliver us,
Lord most high.

We thank you
for the sake of your beloved Son,
whom you called and sent
to serve us and to give us light,
to bring your kingdom
to the poor,
to bring redemption
to all captive people,
and to be forever
and for all mankind
the likeness and the form
of your constant love and goodness.

We thank you
for this unforgettable man
who has fulfilled everything
that is human—
our life and death.
We thank you
because he gave himself,
heart and soul, to this world.

For, on the night that he was delivered up,
he took bread into his hands
and raising his eyes to you,
God, his almighty Father,
he gave thanks
and broke the bread
and gave it to his friends
with the words:

Take and eat,
this is my body for you.
Do this in memory of me.

He also took the cup
and, giving thanks to you, said:
This cup is the new covenant in my blood
shed for you and for all mankind
so that sins may be forgiven.
Every time you drink this cup,
you will do it in memory of me.

So whenever we eat of this bread
and drink from this cup,
we proclaim the death of the Lord
until he comes.

Therefore, Lord our God,
we present this sign of our faith
and therefore we call to mind
the suffering and death of your Son,
his resurrection from the dead,
his entry into your glory,
recalling that he
who is exalted at your right hand
will intercede for us
and that he will come
to do justice to the living and the dead
on the day that you have appointed.

Send us your Spirit
who is life, justice, and light.
O God,

you want the well-being of all men,
not their unhappiness
and not death.
Take all violence away from us.
Curb the passion
that makes us seek each others' lives.
Give us peace on earth
by the power of Jesus Christ,
your Son here among us.
We ask and implore you
to grant us this.

Then your name will be made holy,
through him and with him and in him,
everywhere on earth and here and now,
and forever and ever.
Amen.

Let us pray
to God our Father
with the words
that Jesus has given us:

Our Father, who art in heaven,
hallowed be thy name.
Thy kingdom come.
Thy will be done,
on earth, as it is in heaven.
Give us this day our daily bread,
and forgive us our trespasses,
as we forgive those who trespass against us,
and lead us not into temptation,
but deliver us from evil.
Amen.

This is the forgiveness
of our sins.
This is the body,
broken for you.
Take and eat
and may the peace of God
be with you all.
Amen.

2.

Lord our God,
we thank you that we have been born,
that we exist, with difficulty, but full of joy,
that, within living memory, we have touched your heart
and that we are your heaven and your earth.
You, who have called the stars and determined
    their number,
you also call each one of your people by name.
You know us from afar,
God both far and near.
You are the light of our eyes.
You promise us freedom, life overflowing,
and we keep you to your word,
Lord our God.
We call you with the voices you have given us,
worshipping you with these words:

Holy, holy, holy,
Lord of all powers.
Heaven and earth
are full of your glory.
Come and deliver us,
Lord most high.

You come to deliver us,
God most high.
You have come—
Christ the Lord.

We thank you
because of him
who is our salvation,
the image and likeness
of your love of man,
one of us,
taken from among men,
Jesus of Nazareth,
man of grace,
light of your light.

We thank you
because of him
who went his way
in this world,
giving sight to the blind
and life to the dead,
who did what he could do
for all your people,
and who, on the last night of his life,
presented a sign of love.

He took bread into his hands
and raising his eyes to you,
God, his almighty Father,
he gave thanks
and broke the bread
and gave it to his friends
with the words:

Take and eat,
this is my body for you.
Do this in memory of me.

He also took the cup
and, giving thanks to you, said:
This cup is the new covenant
in my blood,
shed for you and for all mankind
so that sins may be forgiven.
Every time you drink this cup
you will do it in memory of me.

So whenever we eat of this bread
and drink from this cup,
we proclaim the death of the Lord
until he comes.

Therefore we present
this sign of our faith,
Lord our God,
and therefore your Church
on earth
will honor the name
of Jesus crucified
and buried
and risen from the dead.
He, who is your Son
and the Lord of all,
will come
to do justice
to this world,
the dead and the living.

Send your Spirit,
God here among us,
friendship and truth,
life overflowing.
Make us free
from anxiety and bitterness,
free for everyone
who is our neighbor,
so that our hands
may build up peace—
houses of peace
for our children.
Hasten the time
when your future is established,
the new creation
where you are our light,
all in all.

Then your name
will be made holy on earth,
through Jesus Christ,
with him and in him
for ever and ever.
Amen.

Let us pray to God our Father
with the words that Jesus has given us:

Our Father,
who art in heaven,
hallowed be thy name.
Thy kingdom come.

Thy will be done,
on earth, as it is in heaven.
Give us this day our daily bread,
and forgive us our trespasses,
as we forgive those who trespass against us,
and lead us not into temptation,
but deliver us from evil.
Amen.

Does not the cup that we bless
give communion with the blood of Christ?
Does not the bread that we break
give communion with the body of Christ?
Because the bread is one
we all form one body,
for we all share in the one bread.
Take, then, and eat of this bread,
and may the peace of our Lord Jesus Christ
be with you always.
Amen.

3.

We lift up our hearts to you,
Lord most high, holy God.
We thank you—accept our words,
preserve us and hear our prayer.

You come and deliver us,
you give space and freedom to people,
you make the sun rise over good and bad alike.
You have given the earth into our keeping,
you have created us as man and woman,

as people standing shoulder to shoulder,
to live in care and trouble,
in joy and sorrow, but always towards you.

Blessed are you, the God of the powers,
and blessed is he who comes in your name,
Jesus Christ, your Son in this world,
our shepherd until we die,
our example from day to day,
so that we may do what he did,
so that we may become new people,
bread and peace for each other.

We thank you for the sake of him
who, on the night before he suffered and died,
fulfilled everything, became love
and took our bread into his hands,
broke it, and gave it to his friends
with these words:
Take and eat, my body for you.
Do this in memory of me.

He also took the cup
and, giving thanks to you, said:
This is the new covenant in my blood
that is shed for all of you
so that sins may be forgiven.
Every time you drink it,
you will do it in memory of me.

That is why we have come here,
called by you and touched by your gospel.
That is why, Lord our God,

we present this sign of our faith,
proclaim his death until he comes
and bear witness to his life.
He was raised up by you,
the first-born, the new creation,
he was glorified in you
and is concealed in you.

Let us now share in his life.
Send your Spirit over us,
sustain us and keep us alive, God,
give us hope.
Let it be seen in your Church
that you are not a God of the dead
and do not put our trust to shame.
Be worthy of faith
and grant us peace.

Through Jesus Christ, with him, and in him,
we are your people and you are our Father
now and for ever and ever.
Amen.

4.

*To be sung
by the celebrant,
choir, and people*

Celebrant to the people
Peace to you from God our Father,
who has made us,
and from Jesus his Son
and from the Holy Spirit,

who calls in us and breathes in us,
who lives in us.

Choir
It is our honor, it is our safety
to speak your name and stand before you,
listening, waiting, and praying,
Lord our God.

Celebrant
O holy Father, the hour has come—
glorify your Son here among us.

Choir
You called the light into being,
you established the earth,
you fashioned man and gave him life
and placed eternity in our hearts.
You look for us when we are lost—
you have found us,
seen us, taken and glorified us
in Jesus, your servant.
To him you have given the power
to give to all people
life that is everlasting.

All
And this is that everlasting life—
to know you, the one and trustworthy God,
and him whom you have sent,
Jesus, your servant.

Celebrant
We thank you for this unforgettable man.

He is living, the beginning and the end,
the first to be born from the dead,
light of the world,
the first-born of all your creation.
He became the least among men,
bread broken and passed from hand to hand,
and he has given us this sign of his love.

All
On the evening before his suffering and death,
he took bread into his hands
and raising his eyes to you,
O God, his almighty Father,
he blessed you, broke the bread
and gave it to his disciples
with the words:
Take and eat, this is my body for you.
Do this in memory of me.

Celebrant
He also took the cup
and, giving thanks to you, said:

All
This cup is the new covenant in my blood
shed for you and for all mankind
so that sins may be forgiven.
Every time you drink this cup,
you will do it in memory of me.

Celebrant
So whenever we eat of this bread
and drink from this cup,
we proclaim his death until he comes,

we testify that he rose again for us,
we believe, Lord God,
that you sent your Spirit
so that we might do what he has done.

All
We ask you,
send us the power and the disposition
that were in him
and let your Holy Spirit move us
so that we may become like this man
and that we may be your peace in this world,
justice, light of your light,
a new beginning of love.

Celebrant
We ask you this
through him and with him and in him,
who has gone before us to you
and who has told us to pray to you
with these words:

All
Our Father, who art in heaven,
hallowed be thy name.
Thy kingdom come.
Thy will be done,
on earth, as it is in heaven.
Give us this day our daily bread,
and forgive us our trespasses,
as we forgive those who trespass against us,
and lead us not into temptation,
but deliver us from evil.
Amen.

Celebrant to the people
Come, for everything is prepared.
The body of Christ will preserve you
and may the blood of Christ come over us.

> *The bread is broken and shared*
> *and the cup is handed round.*

5.

What shall we say to you, our God—
you who are called:
God of people?
You are no other
than he who said:
I shall be there for you.

You lead us through night and desert
to a land of rest,
a city of peace.
You wait for us
until the day we die.
You know and call
the beaches of the earth,
the banks of heaven,
the sun, the seed in the womb,
the heart that falters,
the mourner who grieves,
the dying, the living.
All the living
you call by their names,
so that they may rejoice in you.

You are always,
you are every moment,

since living memory
you are.

We are of dust
and our days hay and grass,
but you do not deny
the work of your hands.
With our voices we reach up
to you, who live forever.
Do not turn away from us
when we call to you:
holy, holy, holy.
Blessed are you,
known and loved
because of him,
Jesus of Nazareth,
your Son.

He came, invested with your name,
inspired by your name,
and, on the night before he suffered and died,
he fulfilled everything
and became your man.

He took our bread into his hands,
broke it, and gave it to his friends
with these words:
Take and eat,
my body for you.
Do this in memory of me.

He also took the cup
and said:

This is the new covenant
in my blood,
that will be shed for you
so that all sins may be forgiven.
Do this in memory of me.

Therefore, Lord God,
with bread and wine
we remember, until he comes,
his death and resurrection.
Accept this sign of our faith
and send your Spirit down over us.

You have called us
from far and near.
You have made us—
great and small,
each one of us different
in heart and face,
but all of us your people.
We ask you, then,
make new people of us
who hear your voice
with living hearts.
Do this today
and never take your hands
away from us.

We ask you this
through Jesus your Son,
with him and in him,
now and forever.
Amen.

6.

The choir and people sing
Psalm 91

Whoever lives in the shelter of the most high God
and spends the night in the shadow of God almighty—
he says to the Lord: my refuge, my stronghold,
my God, in you I put all my trust.

He sets you free from the nest of the birdcatcher,
he keeps the plague of evil from you,
he will cover you with his feathers,
under his wings you will find safety.

In the dead of night you have nothing to fear;
neither dread in the daytime a stab in the back,
nor fear the plague that stalks in the darkness—
no fever will ruin you in the heat of day.

Although a thousand fall at your side,
ten thousand go down before your eyes,
it will not touch you, your God is faithful,
he is a shield, a wall round about you.

You have only to lift up your eyes
to see how wickedness is avenged.
Then you say: "The Most High is my refuge,"
and you will be at home with him.

No disasters will happen to you,
no pestilence will come close to your tent.

He has sent his angels out,
to guard you at every step you take.

They will bear you up on their hands—
no stone will hurt your feet on your way.
You will plant your foot on the head of the lion,
you will trample on the snake, you will kill the dragon.

"Yes, if he clings to me I will rescue him,
I will make him great, for he holds on to my Name.
If he calls, I will answer. In anguish and need: I with him,
I will make him free and clothe him with glory.

He shall live to be full of years.
He shall live to see my rescue."

> *Then follows the prayer*
> *in which Jesus of Nazareth*
> *is seen as the one*
> *in whom the words of Psalm 91*
> *were fulfilled.*

We thank you, God almighty,
and we bless you.
You cannot be thought of
or named.
You are a stranger,
a friend,
the most high.
You are our shield
and our trust,
our refuge,
the shadow of safety.

We thank you

that we may live to see your glory,
that we may live to see your rescue
in Jesus of Nazareth, the son of men,
whom you called and predestined
to be the angel of your name,
the messenger of your faithfulness.

He went out into this world
and gave himself to the very end,
a servant without form or distinction.

As a sign of the disposition
that was in him,
he took bread into his hands,
broke it, and gave it to his friends
with these words:
Take and eat,
my body for you.
Do this in memory of me.

He also took the cup with wine
and told us:
This is the cup of the new covenant,
my blood that is shed
for you and for all mankind
so that sins may be forgiven.

Therefore, God,
because he did this,
because he became so small,
even as far as the cross,
because he clung to you
and called you, in anguish and need,

you answered him,
rescued him and made him great
and clothed him with your glory.
He will live to be full of years.

Accept what we are doing here
in memory of him
and arouse in us the power and the disposition
that were in him.
Rescue us too,
rescue this world from death,
prevent the disasters that threaten us,
and keep the plague of war from us.

Send your Spirit,
who can protect this world in the dead of night.
Bear us up in your hands
and give us your peace,
so that, through Jesus, with him and in him,
we shall become your sons,
born again.

Therefore we pray to you, God,
and come to you now
with the words that Jesus has given us,
saying:

Our Father, who art in heaven,
hallowed be thy name.
Thy kingdom come.
Thy will be done,
on earth, as it is in heaven.
Give us this day our daily bread,

and forgive us our trespasses,
as we forgive those who trespass against us,
and lead us not into temptation,
but deliver us from evil.
Amen.

7.

*Not to be said,
only to be sung.*

Choir
Whom shall we worship and believe
and who is worth our words
and greater than our hearts?
If there is a God who loves men,
what is his name?

Celebrant
You, who know what is in us
and understand what never can be said,
hear our souls that wait and pray
and turn so restlessly
in search of you.

All
You, with your name unnamable, God,
word, incalculable,
dream folly power freedom,
you who go your way unseen,
God of strangers no one,
God of people running fire
you unheard of in this world—
be worthy of faith here and now
or just for one moment,

open the doors of your light
and let us see you.

Celebrant
Open the doors of our hearts,
unravel the cords that bind us,
powers of darkness despair violence.
You who are called liberator, why
must we be slaves,
servants of war,
why are we caught in each others' hands,
people who beat and are beaten,
people who kill and die.

All
If it is not a dream, a lie
what has been told us—
that there will be good land,
a city of trees like a garden
with houses for everyone,
let us then go there
and place a table in front of us
and give us bread
that feeds like a body.

Celebrant
If there is a way to you,
a man,
direct our feet then,
give us that man.

Choir
If it is he, Jesus of Nazareth,
if there is no one else to expect

than he who gave his whole soul,
was poured out like water,
a lamb slaughtered,
piece of bread broken, cup of wine drunk,

All
If, then, that is life for this world,
give us, around this bread and this cup,
the strength to be him,
and that, through us, in us,
your name may be lived, made holy,
your kingdom of peace will come,
bread of justice,
people for people,
your will is done,
new heaven, new earth—
open that door
that no one can close.

Celebrant
If you are the God
who loves men,
open us then to you.

8.

Celebrant to the people
Open your hearts
and pray with me
and peace
be with all of you.

Choir
You speak to people

throughout all ages
in many languages
in visible things
and what cannot be seen.
You look for us
in heaven and earth.

All
We bless you now
because you have once
and for all spoken
in one of us,
who was born of you,
for all generations
and became flesh,
dust of the earth,
Jesus of Nazareth.

Celebrant
He became man,
everyone, Adam,
in this world which is
always the same
of almost-people
and groping hands,
world of deaf ears
and of armed peace.

Choir
He was fire and light,
living water,
vine strongly growing,
word like a way,

but he was stripped bare
and extinguished.

All
And Jesus said:
I have come to you
in order to be
drunk like a sea,
to become bread,
seed in the ground.

The Celebrant
And therefore he
emptied himself
for friend and stranger,
for good and evil,
and at his wits' end
and for eternity
could and can do
nothing else
but be our God,
God for all men
in this our world.

All
We are that man
to whom he says:
this is my body,
living bread;
this is my blood,
my soul for you—
do to each other
what I have done.

Celebrant
You who are different,
unknown and calling,
eternal distance,
you who in Jesus,
this son of men,
became our Father—
we bless you now
and we admire you.

Choir
And in this bread
here in our hands
we receive him
in groping faith—
your name, your son,
and our own life
in joy and sorrow.

All
Let us perceive
in this small sign
here in this place,
listening, singing,
behind the words,
that it will one day
be made true—what we
expect from you
in hope and fear:
that the day will come
when we shall speak to you
as man to man

till nothing remains
but seeing and silence
and being forever.

Celebrant to the people
Open your hands
and take this bread
and peace
be with all of you.

9.

You who have given us
the earth to live in,
you who see the world—
you know that we are unable
to achieve peace and justice,
yet you still call us
by our names,
each one of us,
to do justice
and to be good.

We pray to you
for all your people,
great or small,
created by you
and the same everywhere,
yet always at war
with each other.

We pray to you
for those who are most defenseless,

for children and poor people
and those who are ill-used.
We pray for these
and for refugees,
the sick, the hungry, and the dying,
for people without a future
and those who have to suffer greatly.
You know what is in us.

Not for death, but to live—
that is why you made us.
Send us your Spirit,
give us the power
to become people,
whatever it may cost us.
May we not chase after emptiness,
run away from the truth,
forget your name.
May we hasten the coming
of your kingdom
and accomplish your will,
share the bread of this world
with each other
and be quick to forgive
all the harm that is done to us.

Praying to you,
our eyes are fixed
on Jesus of Nazareth,

who made your name holy,
accomplished your will,
became bread and wine for us,

food and joy
and the forgiveness of sins.

On the night that he suffered and died,
he said to us:
Take and eat and drink,
this is my body
and this is my blood.
Do this in memory of me.

Blessed are you,
living God,
because of him
the son of men,

word and form
of your glory,
image and likeness
of your faithfulness.

He was humbled
and was broken
but was exalted
in your light.

He was heard.
He was lived.
He will come
into this world.

He will give us
a new name.
He is our way
through death.

We recognize him
and we proclaim him
here in the breaking
of the bread.

10.

Here in this place,
we who are people
in this universe
of hunger and thirst,
of clods and darkness,
of just happiness,
light on the water,
the sky open—
in this world
I speak you,
although no words
are ordinary enough
to name you,
small and invisible.

You are not a man,
not a hand, not eyes
blind in the sea,
stone in the water,
no god, no spirit,
no power—just do
something to us
if you dare and exist,
who are you and where?
I suppose you are
right here among us
or everywhere.

Just name them then,
countries and towns
where life is not worth living.

If you exist,
then you are all:
the living, the dying;
everywhere, nowhere;
refugee, stranger.
Then your life must
again and again
be like that
of that man
from Nazareth
who was killed
for no reason
by other men.
Then you are as
insignificant
as he was,
as this little piece
of bread that does not
appease our hunger,
Then you do not
take death off
our shoulders
and nobody
is made better by you.

But if you exist,
and whatever
your name is,
I will let you

exist and simply
be what you are,
just like everyone
who breathes and looks
and has no defense
against the things
that just happen
whether there is no God
who sees everything.

You give no answer
of course; you have no
voice that joins in
in our language.
I who say this,
who am speaking to you
and cannot do otherwise
because I have heard
of you, some time,
because I hear you
in people people
and in myself—
I should like to do
something, understand you,
sit down on your
doorstep, endure
the silence that you
are, that we are.

Prayer

1.

PRAYER is naïve. It is waiting for someone who never comes.
. Asking for something or someone who is not there.
    If there is a god who loves man,
    let him speak. Now.
This is what the poet Seneca says in his tragedy *Thyestes*.
Repeat it after him:
    If there is a god present here,
    let him answer me. Now.
No answer. No one gets up in the circle of people and that
is a good thing too.

Prayer is monotonous. Always the same words—have
mercy on us, give us peace, take pity on us. The whole of
world literature sings the same song, is simply a variation
on that one theme of love and death, hoping for mercy,
longing for peace. There is very little that all of us can
say and think and hope, but we are able to vary that one
little theme and give it different shades of meaning in
endless repetitions. The medieval story of Tristan and

40

Isolde begins with the words, "Will you hear about love and death." Anyone who has anything to say or to sing just varies and repeats these words in different keys— even now.

Praying also is playing variations on that familiar theme Be merciful to us, be present here, what is your name.

People pray to each other. The way one man says "you" to another, respectfully, intimately, desperately. The way someone says "you" to you, hopefully, expectantly, intensely, his voice seeking or caressing. It may be that praying to God grew out of this way that people have of speaking with each other.

2.

How did mankind come by it? Where did this phenomenon originate? Praying is simply a matter of course in all the holy books of all religions. It is simply there—either it came suddenly or it has always been there.

O our mother earth, O our father heaven,
we are your children.
The sacrifices you ask for we offer
with bent backs.
Weave us a garment of radiant sunlight,
the white dawn the warp,
the red evening the woof.
Let the murmuring rain be the fringe
and the rainbow the hem.
Weave us a garment of radiant sunlight.
We want to walk where the birds sing.
We want to walk through the green grass,
O our mother earth, O our father heaven.

This prayer of an Indian tribe in North America simply exists. There are words that are called "prayer." The pious, meager words of the "Hail Mary"—pray for us sinners, now and at the hour of our death. The fashionable, refined, and carefully weighed out formulas of the much praised and untranslatable *Missale Romanum*.

There are people who—on paper or with their faces hidden behind their hands—talk with God, pray, and it gives the impression of being a decent way of indulging in fancies or complaining about yourself. There was once a certain Augustine who, in his famous *Confessions*, directed philosophy and chatter against his God. He was thoughtful, friendly, grandiose, or wretched, saying exactly what he felt at the moment and without a trace of shame, quite carried away by his own words. One is almost tempted to envy him. As in this passage:

"I was sent to school to learn how to read and write, things the usefulness of which I had no idea. All the same, every time that I was slow to learn, I was beaten. God, my God, what misery I suffered there and how deceived I was!

"We did, however, come into contact, Lord, with people who prayed to you. From them we learned—while we were, to the best of our ability, forming an impression of you—that you were someone great and powerful, able to hear us and to come to our help, even without revealing yourself to our senses. And it is true that, even as a small boy, I began to pray to you, my refuge and my help, and, calling on you, I lost all control of my tongue and, although I was a little person, I asked you with no little fervor that I might not be beaten any more at school."

Praying intimately and enjoyably—a lot of people must

have tried and indeed learned to do this until they lost the ability and could not believe any more.

Prayer is a fact that occurs, in history, in our own district—a priest who says mass every day on his own (perhaps because he has been doing it for the past forty years) or a woman who goes on her knees across the square and up the steps at Fatima and is photographed, in her foolishness, and gets into the newspapers. "To go round the earth seven times, if necessary on your hands and knees," Ida Gerhardt wrote in her poem *The Dead One*. "Praying is breaking in and pushing through in secret," Karl Jaspers wrote, "it is only when a man is completely isolated and deeply threatened that he dares to do it." And what did Martinus Nijhoff mean when he wrote:

Prayer is the sense of this cautious encounter.
O, the whisperings, the comfort of greeting—
his word becoming flesh, we embrace it
in our flesh becoming word, in our prayer,
if, to our originally fearful voice,
his present silence replies.

Words that exist, printed as though it is true, legible. What, then, is their real content? Are they thought out or experienced, made or born? What is prayer?

3.

Prayer is simply a matter of course in the Bible. So much so that there was simply no word for "pray" to begin with in Israel. Praying was calling, rejoicing, laughing, crying, reviling, imploring, according to how one felt. There are hardly any fixed rites, specially privileged places, or

strictly prescribed times of prayer. Everything is allowed
—this is the strongest tendency in this people's relation-
ship with their God. There is no special language for
prayer, sacred and sublime, no standardized jargon, con-
sciously simple or formally polite—you can pray in any
posture and with any voice. Because the God of Israel is
different from all other gods, not a god who compels and
makes demands and uses force, not a "mother earth and
father heaven" to whom we bring our sacrifices with our
backs bent and our eyes cast down. He is space and freedom and you can say anything to him. No word is too
uncouth or too spontaneous for him. You can play with
him, flatter him, overcome him, or go as far with him as
you want to and as you have to, like Abraham when he
bargained with him about Sodom and Gomorrah (50, 40,
20, or 10 just men). You can pour out your heart to him
and rage against him, as Job did:

I will not keep my mouth shut.
I must express the bitterness of my soul—
you force me to it.
Am I the sea, or a sea monster, perhaps,
to be locked up and guarded by you?
There is no comfort for me,
even when I am in bed—
you come to scare me
with dreams and visions of terror.
I would rather be strangled.
What is man,
that you are so interested in him,
that you give him such attention,
that you look every morning
to see if he is still there,
that you test him every moment?

When at last will you look away from me
or let me alone
till I swallow my spittle?
What have I done to you,
prying watcher of men?

What do God and man do to each other and what is
man? The psalms of Israel are always seeking an answer
to that question, but there is no one answer, no clearly
definable experience of the covenant. "What, then, is
Man, that you remember him, the son of Adam, that
he touches your heart," says Psalm 8. " 'My God,' I call
all day—you are silent, I call through the night, and you
just let me call," says Psalm 22. But what does become
clear in these strange, foreign songs is how a man learns
to live with these questions, with that God, with himself,
and through what depths of despair and impotence he
has to go because of this. What becomes visible in the
prayer of the psalms is the movement known as faith.

Psalm 42 is a nervous, almost neurotic poem full of
inner conflict, for and against—I thirst for God, the living God, and always I hear them saying: "Where is your
God?" A vision of longing and fear, of nearness and deser-
tion at the same time—all your breakers are dashing
against me, waves are sweeping over me—I hear them
calling: "Where is this God of yours?"—why do I go
about in rags, harassed and abased—but why so discour-
aged, why rebellious? I will wait for God. And in that to
and fro, the heart at last comes to rest; slowly and after
a series of shocks, the last word, at least for the time
being, is reached—you are my safety, Lord, you are my
God.

In Psalm 69 man assaults the cliffs with prayer, his
voice breaking.

Save me, God, I am up to my neck in the water,
I am sinking, the mud is sucking me down—
water, only water, the current drags me along.

Water is death, the abyss in which one is totally lost.
Then the image changes and people become death.

Because I have trusted in you they are laughing at me,
yes, I have lost my face and become a stranger.

Then the images change again—the sea of contempt, water
as a grave, God's depths like a mother's womb. Abyss calls
to abyss—God, if I have to be lost, let me be lost in you.

Then pull me up from the mud, or am I to drown
in this contempt, in this abysmal water?
Let the flood, the precipice never devour me,
let the mouth of the grave not close over me.
In your love, God, I would be secure,
as in a mother's womb—after all, I am yours.
Do not turn away, do not be such a silent God.

In this psalm, calling to God is being thrown back on
yourself, experiencing the impossibility of God, descend-
ing into yourself, into the pit that you are, the abyss of
becoming fear, being nowhere, alienating, and hating.
This prayer hates and reviles—enemies both without and
within and everything that tears a man to pieces and rises
up in his own heart and breaks out against himself.

You know them by name, all those who rise up against me.
Strike them with blindness, cripple their loins forever,
pour out your curses upon them like so many flames,
just let them burn in the blazing fire of your anger.
Lord, wipe out their names from the book of life.

This is, of course, a famous passage from a psalm of
cursing one's enemies, and when we read it we think our-

selves superior to all this, because of our civilization and
our New Testament, our advanced humanity, and so on.
The man who dared to pray this psalm for the first time
unmasked himself—he saw and knew, this is me, tor-
mented, harassed, aggressive and in need; all of this is in
me. He was a man who—praying? reviling? crying?—
left his illusions behind him and came to the truth. Having thus emptied himself and having set all his misery
free in prayer from the clutch of fear, his feelings can
come to rest, purified and liberated, and he can experience
that there is still more than this—that he is greater than
hatred and fear, that God is deeper than death and will
accept him as he is. The last words of Psalm 69 express
this as an experience of resurrection: you will save me—
all who are looking for God will come to life—he will
come to rescue his people. What is experienced and expressed in this prayer is the history of the people of
Israel.

4.

Jesus of Nazareth recognized himself in the psalms. From
"why have you abandoned me" to "into your hands I com-
mend my spirit," he went the way of faith, he went
through everything that is expressed in Psalm 22: I cry
out, and you stay far away—I am no longer a man but a
worm—you are my God from my mother's womb onward
—I am poured out, wasted like water—they have pierced
my hands and feet—I will tell my brothers about him:
"never has he turned his back upon me"—the ends of the
earth will remember it—our God is faithful.

The change from being lost to being rescued, from death
to life, is "between the lines" in this psalm. It is not a

moment, it cannot be described, it is not a literary image, it "is" not there. This is similar to the detailed description in the gospel of Jesus' death, but lacks any moment at which death changes into life, the "moment" of the resurrection. All that is recorded is the fact that it happened and how it was made credible in the lives and testimony of men.

The gospel says several times that Jesus prayed, in the loneliness of the hill country, and that, like Moses, he went up the mountain to speak with God. "He went up the mountain to pray there," Luke says, "and while he was praying his face changed." His form was glorified and his skin became like light. We see this in the paintings of the Flemish primitives. In their singing angels and visionary mystics, we see that a man's face can sometimes change when he is praying.

In all the gospels, this story of the glorification on Mount Tabor—where Jesus spoke with Moses and Elijah about his death, his exodus—is a story of resurrection. Only Luke describes the moment on Tabor as an experience of prayer. Is what we call, so inadequately, "resurrection" perhaps an experience of prayer? The fact that he lives is only known by people who pray, and the name that he is given as the risen one, the Lord, was first handed down to us as a prayer: *maranatha,* come, Lord, come— that prayer, that cry which is one of the earliest testimonies to faith in the resurrection.

Prayer is an experience of resurrection. Every prayer in the Bible, however ragged and desperate it may be in its beginning, grows towards a moment when man can breathe again: you are my safety, Lord, you are my God. A man has the power of resurrection when, in prayer, he reaches the point where he can believe that it is good, still good in spite of everything: this is me, I am like this and not like that, inadequate and empty, no more than this; I may be futile, my life may be short, but I am still alive, I exist, I am accepted as I am, I am allowed to be there. Incomprehensible, daring words are born in the ecstasy and despair of prayer. We are risen with Christ, Paul says, our life is concealed with Christ in God. The God who accepted Jesus will also accept and rescue us. This light can shine for us in prayer and we will recognize ourselves in him and once more find our name, ourselves. The empty, fleeting word "man" once again becomes my own name, just as, in the language of the Bible, the word "man," *adam,* is *the* proper name par excellence. I am a man, a son of men. Delivered up into the hands of men, but more unique than anything that men can make with their hands and break in me. I was born, not made, I am a man like him, I am accepted, a son of God. If I know that—sometimes only for as long as a word—then my prayer has been heard.

5.

Praying is speaking God's name, or rather, seeking God's name. What is your name?—the eternal question that comes back again after every answer. Praying is trying to turn that empty, fleeting little word "God" into a name that means something to me, to us, now. After all, if I say "God," I am really nowhere at all. I have to make the long journey from "God," a cliché, meaningless and boring, to "my safety, my God," the proper name in which echoes of the whole of his history with mankind can be heard. That is praying.

A name is more than a word. A person's name is full

of history. A person's name at once calls to mind facts
and experiences, joy and sorrow, misunderstandings.
When I speak the names of my friends, I am at once
reminded of what I have in common with them, of what
binds us together. People sometimes say of a dead person: when I speak his name, he is there. Calling someone
by his name is giving him the chance to become himself,
addressing him as he is. You can humiliate a person,
isolate him, and even dehumanize him if you never speak
his name but always make do with a nickname or some
corruption of his real name or if you just call out to him.

Praying is blessing, praising, giving honor to God (so
the psalms say)—the very opposite to humiliating him
—calling God by his name, giving him the chance to
become himself, "our God."

I want to call you, God, by your name,
as truly as I live.

This is how Psalm 104 begins. And then everything is
brought in—the first hour of creation when "the water
was still above the mountains" and then the grass and
crops growing in the fields and the wild goats jumping in
the mountains and then man, laboring until darkness
falls. And, surveying the whole world like this, the author
of this song hits on the track of God's name:

And all this, God, is your own work—
your wisdom speaks from so many things,
your power of creation fills our earth.

Who is God? What is his name? He is what he does
to us. His "power of creation fills our earth." In this psalm
the whole of creation is listed and the whole of God's
history with man is brought up again. Praying like this is
keeping God to his name, reminding him who he is:

"You who have been this and that for us, at this time and at that time, remember what you have done to us and the promise that is implied in it, do not forget who you are, be faithful to yourself. You who called Abraham to leave his own little world and made him fruitful; you who gave your name to Moses and led him with the whole of your people through the sea and the desert; you who took David . . . ; you who gave your name its full force in Jesus of Nazareth—you will then do for us . . ."

Prayer is memory, recalling, rethinking, telling the story again and again, in hope and admiration. It is only in that story of how people fared with him that justice is done to the name of God and that we recognize and remember what we have, unknowingly perhaps, experienced with God, and how the little word "God" has become a name for us.

The Bible, preaching, liturgy are simply memory—by recalling and rethinking, proclaiming and reciting "the word that has happened." Psalms, song, and prayer are a condensation of this in the form of a hymn. They ask and implore that what was once true may now be true for-ever, that he may continue to be a God of people. And then our asking changes into selfless admiration and adoration that he is this: "we bless your name."

6.

When he was about thirty years old, Isaiah, a priest serv-ing in the temple at Jerusalem, had the ecstatic experience of being called to be a prophet. The God of Israel ap-peared to him as a king on his throne and above the throne were seraphs—firebirds, we might call them—praying in the air. It was from them that he heard that vertical and relentless song of praise, that blessing of

God's name, which has been handed down to us and which we still call out today in our liturgy as though we too had tongues of fire and were angels ourselves: "holy, holy, holy."

Holy. A difficult, obscure word encountered in many different and odd combinations—Holy Spirit, Holy Father, Holy See, holy or sacred cow. (And, in the case of the "sacred" cow, we all know with absolute certainty that the word "holy" or "sacred" is misplaced—a cow is a cow and a sacred cow disrupts the whole social and economic structure of a country like India with its hundred million inhabitants.)

The original meaning of holy, in the earliest parts of "holy" Scripture, was something like brilliant, gleaming, blinding light. Later, and in Latin, it meant separate, exceptional, unique, strange, different. In English, it is connected with whole and wholeness, hale, heal, health.

There is enough inside and outside us which we cannot understand—it is too high and too deep. But what is really higher and deeper than we can reach and think is another person—a stranger in his own world, who lives and feels differently and has another name. Whenever another person suddenly begins to gleam and radiate a blinding and alienating light and becomes quite unique in our eyes, as small and as great as he is, or whenever we find health and wholeness in him and can be healthily and wholly ourselves when we are with him, then perhaps we dare to say: this is holy, you are holy to me, you call me, make me, I become another person through you. If another person really appears in our life, as strange and unique and ordinary and near as he is, our minds begin to reel as if we are in a vision and we feel lost. Every person who is bound up with another to the death knows this.

Other, other, other, holy, holy, holy. In the vision that

he had when he was called, Isaiah experienced his God
as the unique other one, so blinding and strange and so
near that he could touch the hem of his garment, as a
God who called him and touched him with fire, a God
who made another person of him, who made him holy.
That is why his mind reeled and he cried out: I am lost.

In the tradition of liturgical prayer, "holy, holy, holy,"
as the blessing of God's name, was connected with the
exclamation "hosanna," which means "come and deliver,"
"liberate." Just as I can experience another person as a
unique opportunity for life, a liberation, precisely because
he is not me and does not have my heart and my voice,
and just as everyone must be rescued by others, so too
can a person in faith and prayer experience his God as a
liberation and call out: come and deliver us, O Other
One, O Holy One. The vision of God's holiness then becomes a prospect of rescue, forgiveness, resurrection; it
becomes a man who is called "God will liberate," Jehoshuah, Jesus.

"Hosanna"—"Jehoshuah," two words from the same
Hebrew root, related to each other like question and answer, hope and fulfillment, prayer and the answer to
prayer.

7.

Prayer is a way of living, not having, asking. It is not com-
peling, not wanting to live from power and possession,
but imploring to be allowed to be. I have to ask for what
is there, things, people, so that they are no longer far
away and nameless and simply present, but become reality assigned to me, given to me. I ask the other person who
loves me: will you love me, may I love you, do you love
me? No one, after all, can have the love of another person

at his disposal. We do not have the sun at our disposal and that is why we can pray for the sun.

Asking is risky. It is entrusting yourself to the silence and the uncertainty of another person, giving him the freedom either to answer or not to answer, to deny or to relativize or to transcend the question in the answer he gives. Asking is the opposite of demanding and the opposite of running away. Anyone who asks opens himself to many possibilities. He makes himself defenseless, but at the same time places himself in that defenseless position, without shame, and says: this is me, I am no more than this, this is what I am hoping for. In the questions I ask I express my consciousness of myself and my conscience.

This attitude towards life sometimes becomes something you can hear and it is sometimes evoked in the circle of praying people by what is known as the "bidding prayers." The liturgical prayers of petition ought to interiorize and purify the questions and the longings we live with. The openness and the subtlety of the form of the prayers and the tone of voice in which they are said ought to suggest that what is involved is an expectation and a care that are far greater than all the details, all the "intentions" that are expressed. The whole community arouses and examines its conscience in the bidding prayers—this world is our sphere, Vietnam and Biafra, they are mine, all war, we are it ourselves. And the one question that lies behind all our formulas of prayer and still remains after all our words are spoken is this: Will we do what we see and will we be what we say? We pray for peace, call upon each other to be human, but the question is: Will we ourselves be men of peace? We pray for those who govern us and in our prayer we call upon

each other to take an active part in politics. We pray for
the poor and the dying and in so doing we wave them
aside, push them out of the Church, and tell each other
who is really involved in this world. We pray for other
people, acknowledge our close ties with them, want to
help and serve them, and yet let them go out of our
hands. And although we are so concerned with this
world and almost lost in this great here and now and con-
stantly defining our questions, we still remain open to the
fact that there is an answer that is different from and
fuller than the one we imagine, that what we are is meaningful.

Our bidding prayers are prompted and directed by a
faith that inspires all prayer: "I have opened a door for you
which no one can close." That is why, in the face of everything that may happen, those who believe dare to say:—
and yet. Just as a demonstration for peace in Vietnam or
against any injustice whatever is a desperate attempt to
remain open to the fact that we, a little crowd of people
are greater and more eternal than that war that just goes
on, so too a bunch of praying people say:—and yet peace
is still possible. Appearances and reason are all against
them in prayer, just as they are against a protest march,
but perhaps, if they did not do it, they would become
choked up and shut up like clams and become war them-
selves.

8.

The closeness of friendship, of someone who loves me,
changes my life and the whole appearance of the world
around me. I live somewhere in a suburban house with a
red roof and a small garden and trees in the street. If I

am lonely and unhappy, even though the physical details remain the same, the house is different from the one in which I experience friendship and love. A woman is dying of cancer, it goes on for months. A man loves her, remains faithful to her, every day. She may well say to him: you have changed my illness. But there is no medical instrument which can register that change in her.

Someone prays for a cure. He calls God close to him, calls on his faithfulness and friendship. The meaning of his illness changes in his prayer, its appearance changes —he himself changes, becomes greater than his fear and pain. He dies, but he dies differently. In the Garden of Olives, Jesus of Nazareth prays: Father, let this cup pass me by. This does not happen and his destiny is fulfilled. History tells us that he had to drink the cup and die. The gospel says that this prayer of his was answered and that he rose again from death.

Praying is asking for this or that, another person, and getting what you did not ask for: the "power" to accept, without any cynicism, that this or that, or the other person, is not given to you. In Psalm 30, a man prays for life (for what use is it to God if he dies, if he is laid in the grave?). "Then you changed my sorrow into joy." The psalm does not say that death was removed from his life. He may have been given more life than he asked for, more than simply being able to breathe, walk, and eat again. Perhaps what he was given was being able to know, wait, and accept. That kind of life and power is called "Holy Spirit" in the gospel. "Will your Father who is in heaven not give the Holy Spirit to those who ask him?" It is said of this Spirit that he will give the earth the freshness of youth.

9.

Praying is more waiting than looking for. Looking for is action and impatience; waiting is attention. Waiting does not give me any guarantee that the one I am expecting will come. Praying does not give me any guarantee that God will come.

Waiting is vague and empty and disinterested: I leave it to the other person to be as he is, to come or not to come. Praying is persisting in the uncertainty as to whether God will come and deliver me or whether he exists for me. Putting up with a gap, looking death in the face.

Waiting is becoming powerless. Psalm 131 says, in prayer:

I have tamed my desires,
my soul has come to rest

like a little child that has drunk
and lies at the breast of his mother;

a little child that has drunk,
so is my soul in me.

Prayer is approaching birth, being silenced. No one can pray without words, because no one exists outside language and everything is dialogue.

What Gerrit Achterberg says in this poem is probably something like prayer:

I can only meet words, no longer you.
But the greeting still goes on, so much

that I have to believe you are listening—
just as I hear your silence in me.

Hearing silence, listening behind the words and for-
getting them, doing nothing and being interior, deeper
than all expression—that is prayer.

Easter Eve

The great Protestant church in Amsterdam,
the Westerkerk.
Everyone who comes in
is given a program
and a candle.

On a platform, beneath the pulpit—
a wide oak table
on which stands
a seven-armed candlestick
with lighted candles in many colors.
The church is sparsely lighted.

Organ music.
Other instruments.

This is how the game begins:
the one who is leading the service
(dressed in dark clothes)
stands in the central aisle
halfway along the church
and makes a sign to the organist
to stop playing.
He then goes on to the platform,
stands behind the microphone
and, with both arms,
makes the gesture of resurrection—

the gesture for the people to stand up.
They all rise.
Two trumpets play
the first bars of the opening song.
Then the leader of the service
begins to sing,
boldly and loudly,
looking at the people
as though he wanted to sell them something:

In the beginning
there was no world.
In the beginning men and women
men and women had not yet been born.

Then the choir joins in
the singing of the opening song
which anticipates
the story of genesis.
the one who is leading the service
steps back and joins one of the rows
of people round the platform.

In the beginning there was no world.
In the beginning men and women
men and women had not yet been born.
In the beginning there were no paths,
cells of fire, the city, and fog.
In the beginning there were no words.
There was no war and no peace and no life,
someone and no one and who and past,
falling and dying. In the beginning
there was the word and the word was with God.
In the beginning there was no answer.
There was no voice in the heads of people.
There was no person in heaven and on earth.
In the beginning God created heaven and earth.

The last line is repeated
polyphonically and if possible
rather ecstatically
by the choir and the people
ad infinitum,
that is to say,
about ten times.

When it has been repeated
a sufficient number of times,
a man comes forward
to read
the poem of creation.
The people sit.

After every verse
the choir and the people
sing a refrain
in which the story
is acknowledged and helped on
and consent is given to it
"from day to day."

THE STORY OF CREATION

In the beginning God created heaven and earth.
The earth was barren and desolate.
Darkness covered the abyss.
God's breath hovered over the water.
God said: Let there be light.
And the light was born.
God saw that it was good, the light.
God made a division between darkness and light.
He called the light day
and he called the darkness night.
So it was evening and morning.

So it was evening and morning,
the first day.

God said:
Let there be a vault in the middle of the water
to divide water from water.
And so it was.
God made the vault
as a division between the water above
and the water below.
And he called the vault heaven.
So it was evening and morning.

So it was evening and morning,
the second day.

God said:
All the waters under heaven
must flow together in one place,
so that dry land may appear.
And so it was.
He called the dry land earth
and the water that had flowed together sea.
And God saw that it was good.
God said:
Now the earth must produce green plants,
crops which bear seed
and fruit trees bearing fruit,
each according to its kind.
And so it was.
The earth produced green plants,
crops which bore seed
and fruit trees bearing fruit,
each according to its kind.

And God saw that it was good.
So it was evening and morning.

So it was evening and morning,
the third day.
God said:
There must be lights
in the vault of heaven,
to make a division between day and night.
They must also serve as signs
indicating days and years
and determining the season.
They will be there as lights
in the vault of heaven
to give light to the earth.
And so it was.
God made the two great lights—
the greater light to govern the day,
the smaller light to govern the night—
and then the stars.
God gave them their place
in the vault of heaven
to give light to the earth,
to govern the day and the night,
to make a division between darkness and light.
And God saw that it was good.
So it was evening and morning.

So it was evening and morning,
the fourth day.

God said:
The water must teem
with living creatures,

and birds must flutter
and fly above the earth
and within the vault of heaven.
And God created great animals in the sea
and all the living things
with which the water teems,
each according to its kind,
and all kinds of winged creatures.
And God saw that it was good.
And he blessed them and said:
be fruitful and multiply
and make the water of the seas full
and the birds must also become numerous on earth.
So it was evening and morning.

So it was evening and morning,
the fifth day.

God said:
The earth will produce living creatures
of all kinds—
cattle, creeping animals,
wild animals,
each according to its kind.
And so it was.
God made the wild animals as they are
and the cattle
and everything that creeps on the earth.
And God saw that it was good.
And God said:
Now we will make people
who will be in our image and likeness.
They will rule over the fish of the sea,
the birds of heaven,

over all animals,
and everything that creeps on the earth.
Then he created man in his own image,
image of God he created them,
man and woman he created them.
And God blessed him and said to them;
be fruitful and multiply
and make the earth full
and conquer it.
Be lord and master
of the fish of the sea,
the birds of heaven,
of all animals
and everything that creeps on the earth.
And God said:
here, I give you
all the crops which bear seed
everywhere on earth
and all the trees bearing fruit—
this is for you to eat.
And to all wild animals
and to all the birds of heaven
and to everything that lives and moves on earth
I give the green plants to eat.
And so it was.
God saw that everything that he had made
was very good.
So it was evening and morning.

So it was evening and morning,
the sixth day.

Thus heaven and earth were completed
with everything and everything.

God's work was completed
on the seventh day
and he rested from his work
on the seventh day.
God blessed the seventh day
and made it holy,
because he rested then from all the work
that he had done.

So heaven and earth were born.
So we were created.
So it was evening and morning,
this day.

So it was evening and morning,
this day.

> *As the tune of the refrain*
> *is repeated*
> *and gradually played out*
> *on the organ,*
> *a man and a woman*
> *come forward.*
>
> *In question and answer*
> *they introduce*
> *the second great story*
> *of this Easter eve.*
> *The man of course*
> *asks the questions*
> *and the woman*
> *gives the answer*
> *that is no answer.*
> *The form of this dialogue*
> *is derived from the conversation*
> *that takes place*

during the Jewish Passover
between the father of the house
and the youngest son.

THE DIALOGUE

The Man
Why is this night
so different from all other nights?
Why are we listening
to what we already know?
Why are we going back
to the beginning?

The woman
So as not to forget
who we are,
so as to see and recognize
and believe
that we are people.

The man
Why is this night
different from all other nights?
Every other night
we go our own way,
but tonight
we are all together
in one place.

The woman
Because we were slaves
but have been called to freedom.

Because we have been rescued
in order to come together.
Because we are called to freedom
on this night.

The man
Why is this night
different from all nights?

The woman
This is the story
of our liberation.

THE STORY OF THE EXODUS

This story, in six episodes,
read alternately
by the woman and the man,
is a collection of fragments
from the book of Exodus,
chapters 1 to 33.

1.

In those days
the people of Israel were living in Egypt.
They were fruitful and multiplied
and became so numerous
that the country was overrun with them.
Then the king of Egypt said:
the people of Israel are more numerous than we are
and threaten to overwhelm us.

Let us deal tactfully with them.
He appointed slave drivers
to keep the children of Israel down
with forced labor.
But the more they were oppressed,
the more numerous they became,
so that men began to fear
the Israelites.
Then the king of Egypt said:
Throw every boy
who is born to the people of Israel
into the Nile,
but let the girls live.

Now there was a man of the tribe of Levi
who had taken a Levitical girl as his wife.
The woman became pregnant and gave birth to a son
and, because she saw that he was a fine boy,
she kept him hidden for three months.
But when she was no longer able to hide him,
she made a basket of rushes,
covered it with pitch,
put the little boy inside it
and placed it among the reeds
on the bank of the Nile.
And when an Egyptian woman went to bathe there,
she found the basket among the reeds.
She opened it
and saw a little boy crying.
She was sorry for him and said:
This must be one of the children of Israel.
She took the child and called him Moses,

because she said:
I have taken him out of the water.

And for many years
the Israelites groaned in their slavery
and their cries rose up to God
and God heard their crying
and remembered his covenant
with Abraham, Isaac, and Jacob.

2.

When Moses had become a man
and was tending his sheep in the desert,
the God of Israel appeared to him
in a flame of fire in the middle of a bush.
The bush was blazing
but it was not consumed.
Moses thought to himself:
I must go a bit closer:
and look at this strange sight.
When God saw him coming closer,
he called to him from the middle of the bush:
Moses, Moses.
He answered: Here I am.

And God said:
Do not come any closer,
but take your shoes off,
for the place where you are standing
is holy ground.
And he went on:
I am the God of your fathers,

the God of Abraham, the God of Isaac,
and the God of Jacob.
Then Moses covered his face,
because he did not dare
to look up at God.

And God said:
I have seen the misery of my people
and have heard them crying to be set free.
That is why I have come down
to deliver them from the power of Egypt.
See, I shall send you to Pharaoh.
You must bring my people out of Egypt.

But Moses said to God:
Who am I to lead the people out of Egypt?
And then he said:
If I go to your people and say:
"The God of your fathers sends me to you,"
they will ask: "What is his name?"
What am I to say then?
God said:
I am who I am, I shall be there for you.
This is what you must say to the Israelites:
"I shall be there" sends me to you,
the God of your fathers has sent me.
This is my name for all time.
This is what I shall be called
from generation to generation.

But Moses said:
Oh Lord, I am not a good speaker.
I never have been able to speak well

and still cannot,
even though you have spoken
to your servant.
Then God said to Moses:
Who gave man a mouth?
Who makes him dumb or deaf?
Who gives him sight
or makes him blind?
Now go—I shall be there,
I shall tell you what to say.

So Moses went to Pharaoh and said:
This is what the God of Israel says to you:
Let my people leave this country.
But Pharaoh replied:
Who is the God of Israel,
that I should obey him?
I do not know any God of Israel
and I will not let you go.
And the same day Pharaoh gave this command:
Make the children of Israel work even harder,
because they are lazy—that is why they say:
Our God has appeared to us.

So the slave drivers flogged
the children of Israel.
Then the children of Israel said to Moses:
May God punish you for it!
You have made us hated by Pharaoh
and he will certainly murder us.
Moses turned to God and said:
Why did you send me?

For, from the moment that I went to Pharaoh
and spoke your name,
the people have been worse off.
You have not rescued your people at all.

*This last line provides
the point of departure
for the following song,
sung by the choir and people
and accompanied by percussion*

THE SONG "HE SAYS HE IS GOD"

He says he is God—
let him appear before us.
What is the use of a name to us?
Let him rise up—let us see him.
Voice from the fire, cloud in the distance
are not enough
for this earth of fragments and smoke
where we are granted no life.

Words and miracles are in abundance
and gods of gold and promises
but not a god like a hand that sets free
someone who does what he says.

You who say that you are our God,
concealed and blinding impossible you,
what keeps you away from people?
Can you endure all the blows
that people endure?
Can you then drink the cup

that we have to drink?
Will you go with us to death?
Words and miracles are in abundance
and gods of gold and promises
but not a god like a hand that sets free
someone who does what he says.

3.

God said to Moses:
I am God. I shall be there for you.
I have certainly heard
the groaning of Israel's children.
I shall set you free
and you will know
that I am your God
and that I save.
I shall perform wonders
in the sight of Pharaoh
and the whole of the people of Israel.

Then he sent darkness down,
it became as dark as the earth,
water was changed into blood
and all the fish were killed.
The country was swarming with frogs—
they overran the king's palace.
He spoke, and there were the gnats.
Hail and fire rained down.
He spoke, and there were the locusts—
not a blade of grass was left.
But Pharaoh hardened his heart
and refused to let them go.

And Moses went to Pharaoh again and said:
This is what the God of Israel says:
At midnight I shall pass through Egypt
and all the first-born will die,
from the first-born of Pharaoh
to the first-born of the slave.
And such a weeping will be heard
throughout the whole country
as has never been heard before
and never will be again.
But no dog will bark
at any of Israel's children,
so that you will know
that our God is a God who sets free.
And boiling with rage, Moses went away
from Pharaoh.

To the children of Israel he said:
This night will be for you
the beginning of freedom.
Let every man
take one lamb for his family
and slaughter it in the evening hours.
Then you must smear
the doorposts and the lintel of your houses
with the blood of the lamb.
And at night you will eat the flesh
with unleavened bread and bitter herbs.
And you must eat it like this—
with a girdle round your waist,
your shoes on your feet
and a staff in your hand.
And you must eat it with great haste,

because on this night God will pass over you.
And the children of Israel did all this.

And at dead of night
God struck down all the first-born
in the land of Egypt.
And Pharaoh and all the members of his court
and everyone in the whole of Egypt
got up that night
and such a weeping was heard
throughout the whole country
as had never been heard before
and was never to be heard again,
for every house had its dead.

But God passed over
the houses of Israel's children,
because the blood on their doorposts and lintels
was a sign to him.
It was still night when Pharaoh sent for Moses
and said:
Leave my country
and go away with that people of Israel.
Take your sheep and cattle with you,
gold and silver and everything you have asked for.
Only see that you get away as quickly as possible.
The time that the Israelites had spent in Egypt
was four hundred and thirty years.
It was a night of vigil for God.

4.

And Israel left Egypt,
the house of slavery,

and God went ahead of them,
by day in a pillar of cloud to show them the way
and by night in a column of fire to give them light,
so that they might carry on by day and by night.
But once the people of Israel had left,
Pharaoh's mood changed and he thought:
What have I done,
letting Israel leave my service?
And he had horses put on his chariot
and summoned his soldiers
and pursued the children of Israel.
And he soon caught up with them.

When the Israelites saw the Egyptians
coming up behind them,
they were crippled with terror
and cried out to Moses:
Were there not enough graves in Egypt?
Why did you take us out
to die in the desert?
Now God said to Moses:
What are they calling to me?
Tell the Israelites to march on,
lift up your staff, stretch your hand out over the sea
and divide it in two, so that the children of Israel
can walk through the sea without wetting their feet.
Then I shall show my glory
to Pharaoh and his army,
to his chariots and horsemen.
Then the Egyptians will know
that I am your God.

And Moses stretched his hand out over the water
and God drove the sea back

with a strong east wind
which blew all night.
And the children of Israel
went right through the sea
without wetting their feet,
because the water stood like a wall
to the right and the left of them.
The Egyptians chased after them
and all of Pharaoh's horses, with his chariots
    and horsemen,
followed them right into the sea.

But early in the morning
God threw the army of the Egyptians into confusion,
making the wheels of their chariots fall off
and slowing down their march.
And the Egyptians cried out:
Let us flee from Israel,
because God is fighting for them against Egypt.
God now spoke to Moses:
Stretch your hand out over the sea
and the waters will flow back.
Moses stretched his hand out over the sea
and, as day broke,
the sea flowed back to its old place
and the water overwhelmed Pharaoh's chariots
    and horsemen.
Not one was left.

Then Moses and the children of Israel,
on the other side of the sea,
sang this song to their God:

> *Someone with a guitar*
> *comes up to the microphone*

and, like a troubadour,
sings Psalm 114.
Halfway through,
the choir and people join in.
The last lines are sung
as a canon.

PSALM 114

When Israel came away from Egypt,
the children of Jacob,
away from a strange and gabbling people,
then the Lord made
of Judah his holy dwelling-place,
his kingdom of Israel.
When the sea saw it, it took to flight,
and the Jordan shrank back,
the mountains and hills, like rams, like sheep,
like lambs, they were jumping.
Sea, what is wrong, that you take to flight?
Why creep away, Jordan?
And mountains, why like rams, like lambs,
why are you jumping?

The Lord of the earth has shown himself,
the God of Jacob,
who changes rocks into springs and pools,
stones into water.

5.

The children of Israel
set out again from the Red Sea,
but when they had been travelling
for three days in the desert,

they began to complain against Moses:
If only we had died in Egypt,
when we sat down with pans of meat
and could eat as much bread as we wanted!
But you have brought us into this desert
to let us starve to death!

God said to Moses:
I will let bread rain down for you from heaven—
you will learn that I am for you.
And in the morning
dew fell all around their tents
and over the surface of the desert
there was a thin, granular deposit,
as fine as hoarfrost.
When the Israelites saw this,
they said to each other:
What is that?
because they did not know what it was.
But Moses said:
That is the bread God gives you to eat.
And they picked it up,
some gathering more, some less.
But when they came to weigh it,
they found that the man who had gathered more
did not have too much
and the man who had gathered less
did not have too little.

And they travelled deeper into the desert
and began once more to grumble against Moses,
saying:
Give us water to drink.

The place was called trial and contention,
because the children of Israel
had disputed with God and put him to the test
by saying:
Is he among us now or is he not?

6.

Fifty days after they had left the house of slavery,
they reached the mountain of Sinai
and they pitched camp around the mountain.
And on the third day, in the morning,
there were peals of thunder and flashes of lightning
and a dark cloud covered the mountain
and the people were frozen with terror.
And Moses climbed up to God
and spoke there with God
and God answered him.
And there Moses stood face to face with God
and spoke with him
as man to man.

And Moses said to God:
You command me to make this people go on
to the country that you have promised,
but you have not told me
whom you will send with us.
And God said:
Must I go with you myself, then,
to satisfy you?
Moses answered him:
If you are not going with us yourself,
do not make us leave this place.

And God replied:
I shall be there for you,
because you have found favor in my sight
and I have chosen you.
And Moses said:
Show me your glory, then.
God answered:
I shall let my glory go past you
and I shall call my name in your ears,
but you cannot see my face,
because no man can see me
and remain alive.

He went on:
Beside me is a place where you can stand on a rock.
When my glory goes past you,
I will put you in a hollow of the rock
and cover you with my hand
until I have passed by.
Then I will take my hand away
and you will be able to see me from behind.
For no one may see my face.

> *The man and the woman*
> *now go back to their places.*
> *The choir divides itself into two,*
> *one half going right through*
> *the people (a path through the sea)*
> *to the other end of the church.*
> *Facing each other,*
> *the two halves of the choir*
> *sing the following litany*
> *to each other.*
> *The people also divide themselves*

into two halves
and join in or remain silent,
according to whether they have breath.

Seven children
go up to the candlesticks on the table.
Each takes a candle
and with it lights the candles
of the people present,
who in turn pass the light on
to those next to them.
During the singing of the litany
all the lamps in the church
should flash on.

The music of this litany—
like almost all the music
that is used in this Easter vigil—
was composed by
Bernard Huijbers.

THE LITANY

Be here among us, light in the midst of us.
  Be here among us, light in the midst of us.
Show your glory for us to see.
  Stir up your power and come to our rescue.

Be here among us, bring us to life.
  Be here among us, flame of our life.
Flame of our life, God in the midst of us,
  Come to our rescue, bring us to life.

Your rescue dawns like the light in the morning.
  Come and appear, be light to our eyes.

God in the midst of us, flame of our life,
Come here among us, bring us to life.
God of the powers, God of people,
Show us your light, bring us to life.

Or are you, God, a God of the dead?
Come here among us, bring us to life.
Or are you, God, no God of people?
Show us your light and make us free.

For you are God, light in the morning.
For you are God, today and tomorrow.
Your covenant will last for a thousand generations.
For you are God, the God of people.

Since living memory you are God.
For you are holy and unseen,
A God so near and yet so far.
You are not God as we think you are.

We cannot find you. You are a stranger.
Your folly, God, is wiser than people,
Your impotence is stronger than people.
For you are God and what is your name?

O holy God, immortal God,
Be here among us, do not let us die.
For what is heaven to me without you?
Give us your name, a sign of life.
Why am I on earth if you do not exist?
Be here among us, show us your mercy,
Be our breath, be in our blood,
Be our future, be our father.

We exist through you, we exist in you,
   And in your light we see the light.
Show us your mercy, for you are God,
   For you are God. Why must we die?

For not the dead will speak of you,
   For not the dead in their silence.
But we, the living, call out to you,
   But we, the living, on this night,
Call out your name and want to see you—
   Waiting for you and without knowing,
We want to see you in this existence.

   All the living are waiting for you.
Open your hand that we may eat our fill.
   Do not turn away, do not let us die.
Do not let us fall back into the dust.
   But send your spirit, and we come to life,
Flame of our life, light of our light—
   Send us your spirit, and we come to life.
Soul of our heart and light of our light,
   Send us your spirit, and we come to life.
Give to this earth the freshness of youth.

   To all your people, everywhere,
To all your people, of every kind,
   With that great number beyond all counting
We call to you: Be here among us,
   On this night, be our God,
In this city, be our peace,
   In our houses, give us peace,
On our tables, the bread of peace,
   And for our children, be here among us.

Light in the midst of us, people of peace,
   How long must we go on waiting for you?

O God, come back and give us peace—
   How long must we go on waiting for you?
O God, come back, restore us to honor,
   Light in the midst of us, bring us to life.
How long must we go on waiting for you?
   Light in the midst of us, bring us to life.
We place our trust in you, living God,
   And would you ever put that trust to shame?

> *The one who is leading the service*
> *now goes up to the pulpit*
> *(or he can simply speak*
> *from the microphone on the platform)*
> *and reads the Easter gospel*
> *in Mark's version.*
> *Everyone stands.*

THE STORY OF THE RESURRECTION

When the seventh day was over,
Mary Magdalen,
Mary the mother of James, and Salome
bought sweet-smelling spices to anoint him with.
And on the first day of the week,
very early in the morning,
just as the sun was rising,
they went to the grave.
They had been saying to each other:
Who will roll the stone away for us
from the entrance to the grave?

But when they arrived there,
they noticed that the stone had already been rolled away.
They went inside the grave
and to their consternation saw
a young man in a white garment
sitting on the right-hand side.
He said to the women:
Do not be afraid.
You are looking for Jesus of Nazareth,
who was crucified.
He is not here.
He has risen.
Look, this is the place
where they laid him down.
Go now and tell Peter and his disciples:
He is going before you to Galilee, your country,
and it is there that you will see him,
as he told you.
The women came out
and ran away from the grave,
overcome by fear and consternation.
And, in their panic,
they told nobody anything about it.

When the gospel has been read,
the candles are extinguished.
Everyone sits down.

The leader of the service
gives a short address.
On Easter eve 1968,
a week after the murder
of Martin Luther King,
the following address
was given.

ADDRESS

He says he is God—
let him appear before us.
What is the use of a name to us?
Let him rise up—let us see him.

Then a few people rise up from their places, as if by
chance, and come forward with—a story, no more than
that, a handful of memories, an ancient testimony, a
dream, which makes this night so different from all other
nights. There was nothing—there was emptiness, no
voice, no fire, no light. And now there is this world, this
city, people who are more darkness than the night and
more light than all the light of flames and lamps and the
sun. We are those people. There was a people in slavery,
without rights and despised, less than nothing. There was
a man who wanted peace and justice—something as simple
as light and space for every man, whether he crawls or
flies, whether he is black or white, a man in Memphis, a
man from Nazareth. And of course he was shot down or
crucified. (And you are thinking perhaps—another time
a man is killed in one way or another . . .)

And now tonight's story, tonight's dream tells us: that
enslaved people, that murdered man is set free, rescued,
has gone through the sea, through death—he has risen.

These words seem hard and impossible to us who are
full of ideas and understanding nothing. He has risen. A
statement like a sea—you cannot walk on it, you cannot
build on it, it runs like water through your fingers. He has
risen. A statement like a mountain—you cannot see

through it, you do not know what lies behind it, you have no idea what it means. Is he here perhaps—a body with eyes that see, with clothes like us? What is it then?

He is not here. He has risen. This statement appears, without joy or rapture, in tonight's gospel. The first people to hear it ran away in fear and consternation and, in their panic, told nobody anything about it.

This panic need not surprise us. It is no wonder. The fact that we people cannot believe this statement and cannot live it out in our lives, that it is powerless and does not kindle a light in us and that we cannot understand it —this is no wonder. Look at any dead person and you can see nothing of that word "resurrection." And look at so many living people in the world—the dullness, the dreary care, the endless routine, the slavery, the violence, and the apparent desire to keep things exactly the same. The fact that people say that nothing new can ever happen, there is no future, no one can come and deliver me, set me free, the fact that people openly yield to becoming stone, the grave—this despair is no wonder.

But the fact that, even so, in this world, hope is still born, the hope that there will be a hand that rescues and sets us free—someone who does what he say—and that this hope has not yet died, is not yet dead even today, and that this hope still does not die with every dead person —that is the wonder.

Here is a city built, full of pieces of desert, and it never rains bread from heaven here. No one reads the dead illusions in your soul. Yet many of us may know the fear that everything—all our waiting for fulfillment, for an answer—may be an illusion. But there are people in this city—we may be those people—who go the way of hope, again and again, and, walking two and two, dare to build houses, love each other, people who are full of cracks and holes and who are no more than the least among people, but who still do not go under, who go on enduring in this life, without hating and without hitting back.

There are cities built everywhere, from Atlanta to Berlin, and people live in them, people who, despite everything, still go on recognizing their deepest dream in that testimony, that gospel about a man who was killed like the least among negroes and was restored to honor by his God. He is not here. He has risen. How many people there must be, here and everywhere, who hope that the story about Jesus of Nazareth will be fulfilled in them. That he who says he is God will be their God.

No one can say: It will happen to me. As though he knows and possesses something. No one has ever seen God. But you can say: I hope so. I, for myself, hope I shall be set free. I hope that I shall be allowed to exist, that someone will come for me, that rocks will change into springs and pools, that there will be a city without death.

> *Everyone stands*
> *and, led by the choir,*
> *sings*

THE SONG OF THE CITY*

Here is a city built
far as the eye can see,
houses and gardens and
men made of light and clay.

* This English version is by Forrest Ingram, S.J.

Houses for men made of
flesh and blood, homes of peace,
safe, yet unsafe, so they
always live bittersweet.

Everywhere hurry, the
traffic goes many ways,
movement and fuss just like
clouds of smoke with no blaze.

Words pass from man to man,
everywhere on this earth,
words that are joy and grief,
words that are death and birth.

Everyone wants someone
else but knows not how to.
Everyone goes his own
way, no one knows where to.

People walk two and two,
cup filled and cupboard bare,
seeking a home that is
safe, that is free of care.

City is man and wife,
rising and back to bed,
people who die every
day yet they don't stay dead.

Living is loving, it
goes down the same old track,
father and son, it goes
on, there's no turning back.

Everywhere life flows be-
tween flat and factory,
flowers and children at
play, lively melody.

Is there a city with-
out death or darkness, or
will the sun some day be
needed by us no more?

> *During the intermezzo*
> *a collection is made,*
> *music is played*
> *and people talk*
> *and blow their noses.*
> *Plates with bread*
> *and a cup with wine*
> *are placed on the table.*
> *The two halves of the choir*
> *join together again.*
>
> *A slight change of scene—*
> *someone brings*
> *the leader of the service*
> *a kind of "prayer cloak"*
> *with which he "clothes" himself*
> *before taking his place at the table.*
> *This is a garment of office,*
> *because what he is now going to say*
> *will be in the name of many people*
> *and of many centuries*
> *and will go far beyond and above himself.*
> *The cloak that is hung around him*
> *means that the community*
> *authorizes him to do this.*
> *He now begins*

THE TABLE PRAYER

If you want to be our God,
the God of these people here,
then be blessed and named,
known and loved.
You are the beginning and the end,
alpha and omega,
today and tomorrow,
the creator of all things—
of our hands and lips,
of our wombs and hearts,
of our bodies standing upright,
of our laughing
and our believing.
On this Easter eve,
this year of our lives,
we call to you
and we thank you
because of your Son,
Jesus of Nazareth,
your image and likeness,
the first-born of your creation
and first-born of all the dead,
man of grace
who has done so much more
than we think.
Even if he had done no more
than simply open
the eyes of the blind,
but had not been
the light of this world—

this would have been enough.
Even if he had simply been
the light of the world,
but had not been
a man here among us,
as mortal
and as unseen
as we are—
this would have been enough.
Even if he had simply been
a man,
but had not become
the least among men,
the servant of us all—
this would have been enough.
But he became our peace,
our spirit and life,
bread of our life—
and on the night
of his suffering and death
he took bread,
broke it
and gave it to his friends
with the words:
Take and eat,
my body for you.
Do this in memory of me.
He also took the cup
and, giving thanks to you, said:
This is the new covenant
in my blood
shed for you
and all men,

so that sins
may be forgiven.
Do this in memory of me.

> *The eucharistic hymn,*
> *which is more or less the same*
> *as that which is found*
> *in the Didache,*
> *is now sung antiphonally.*
> *The melody is taken*
> *from the Gregorian Exultet,*
> *the song of praise sung*
> *before the paschal candle*
> *in the Roman rite.*

All
So whenever we eat of this bread
and drink from this cup,
we proclaim the death of the Lord
until he comes.

Choir
Blessed is he who comes in the name of the Lord,
Jesus Messiah.
Come and deliver us,
O son of David.

Celebrant
Blessed are you, O Lord God, our Father,
because of David, the holy vine,
in which you have let us share
through Jesus, your servant.

All
To you alone is all honor due
forever.

Celebrant
Blessed are you because of the wisdom and the life
in which you have let us share
through Jesus, your servant.

All
To you alone is all honor due
forever.

Celebrant
Just as the bread that we break
was sowed as seed in the earth
and was gathered together to become one,
so bring us together from far and near
into the kingdom of your peace.

All
To you alone is all honor due
forever.

Celebrant
So we pray to you with the words
which Jesus, your Son, has given us:

All
Our Father, who art in heaven,
hallowed be thy name.
Thy kingdom come.
Thy will be done,
on earth, as it is in heaven.
Give us this day our daily bread,
and forgive us our trespasses,

as we forgive those who trespass against us,
and lead us not into temptation,
but deliver us from evil.
Amen.

> *The bread is broken and shared*
> *at ten different places in the church.*
>
> *Music is played.*
>
> *When the plates*
> *with the bread that is left over*
> *are brought back to the table,*
> *the celebrant gives the cup*
> *to those who are sitting*
> *closest to the table*
> *until it is empty.*
>
> *In the meantime,*
> *accompanied by the organ and flutes,*
> *the choir and people sing*

PSALM 126

When from our exile
God takes us home again,
that will be dreamlike.

We shall be singing,
laughing for happiness.
The world will say:
"Their God does wonders."
Yes, you do wonders,
God here among us,
you are gladness.

When from our exile
God takes us home again,
that will be dreamlike.

Then take us home,
bring us to life,
just like the rivers
which, in the desert,
when the first rain falls
start flowing again.

Sow seed in sadness,
harvest in gladness.
A man goes his way
and sows seed with tears.
Back he comes, singing,
sheaves on his shoulder.

When from our exile
God takes us home again,
that will be dreamlike.

> *Then the one who is leading the service*
> *reads the fourth story of this evening*
> *from the Acts of the Apostles*
> *and concludes the service*
> *with a short prayer.*

THE STORY OF THE ASCENSION

In those days, Jesus said to his disciples:
It is not given to you to know the day and the hour
that the Father has appointed on his own authority.
But you will receive power

from the Holy Spirit, when he comes over you,
to be my witnesses in this city
and to the ends of the earth.
After these words, he was lifted up
in front of their eyes
and a cloud took him away from their sight.
While they were staring after him,
two men in white suddenly stood there
and said: Why are you men standing there
looking up at the sky?
This Jesus, who has been taken away from you
into heaven,
will return in the same way
as you have seen him go to heaven.
So they came down from the mountain
and returned to the city.

PRAYER

You know what is in us.
You have always understood
all our words
and you also understand
what can never be said.
Hear our prayer.
Make peace with us.
Do not let violence increase—
in this city,
in America or Vietnam
or anywhere.
Do not let people be killed—
you made us to live.
Rescue our dead,

O living God,
and do to us
what you did
to Jesus of Nazareth,
your Son,
now and forever.

Go in peace now
and may the God
who has ordered everything for the best for us
protect you now and make you strong,
give you what is good for you
and bless you—
the Father, the Son, and the Holy Spirit.

The bells are rung.
Everyone stands and sings

THE SONG OF GOD WHO IS ON OUR SIDE

Our God provides for us
and knows us like a friend.
He gives us all our life
and loves us to the end.
He sent his only Son
to live on earth as man;
that we should be like him
was God the Father's plan.

Christ suffered on the cross,
enduring every pain.
He gave himself for us,

that we might live again.
Though many laughed in scorn
at Jesus crucified,
this was God's clearest proof
that he is on our side.

What can divide us now
from God who is so near?
In death there is no threat,
the future holds no fear.
His faithfulness is sure,
his love will never cease.
He is our Lord and God
and gives us lasting peace.

> *The carillon plays*
> *as the people leave the church.*

The Second Language

No one ever made the words that he speaks and no one ever invented speech himself, just as no one made himself. It is given.

Anyone who can no longer hear and speak, or does not want to, becomes closed, a stranger to everyone. He is nowhere.

Speaking is precarious—people talk around the subject, interrupt, change the subject, do not understand, are silent. Words heal and wound, build up and sow confusion. Words keep my life open, give me a prospect. The word peace, for example, or the word God, or the name of another person. Or a word deprives me of all hope.

As long as human words are spoken
and man lives for his fellow man
—these are the same.

Words "mean" and confirm what men are for their fellow men. The meaning and dimension of what happens appear in the word. Facts become important and can be experienced through words. Words give direction to events.

Why words? The commemoration of the fallen in the war—the living are addressed across their bodies. Why?

To close a gap? To do justice to their living and dying. To remember that they were people. That is why.

As Hans Andreus has said:

And does not man then listen, tensely, anxiously,
with one ear to the ground and one ear in the air,
to all the voices of mankind
and of man's future?

And Gerrit Kouwenaar:

The only despair
is man unexpressed.

How many words does one man hear and speak in one day? How much talking is done every day in that little piece of city and country that I call my own environment? Words are always exchanged wherever there are people.

Language is a house in the universe, the philosophers say, and human existence is established in the word. But how many words are there that do nothing, do not establish or confirm, do not give any direction, do not live? Just words exchanged?

There are two languages in language, two ways of speaking, two levels of linguistic usage. There is a language of clear truths, concepts, and formulas. The language of pure logic, objective information, exact science. Things are as they are, you say what you mean, as precisely as you can and as unequivocally. Speaking then is deciphering a puzzle, defining, prescribing limits. This is this, not that— it is water, not steam, and not ice. Here is here, not there. One is one, 2=2, dead is dead.

A language of terms, a closed whole of carefully ar-

ranged expressions. A language of abstraction and reduc-
tion—every thing becomes a figure, every word becomes
a number. A language of final solutions and unambiguous
answers.

It is a good thing that we have this language—our world
cannot do without it and everyone understands it and
speaks it a little. But we never use it when we want to
pour out our hearts and say what is really in us, hidden
and almost impossible to name. In questions of love and
death and God and man, this first language, this way of
speaking, is not only inadequate, but also dangerous.

But there is also a second language, deep below the
first like a much older stratum, or wide around the first
—"second" insofar as it is the second to be noticed and
appreciated and insofar as it is more defenseless and modest
than the first language. It is the language of what cannot
really be said. The language that you speak so as not to
have to be completely silent. The language of emotion
and ecstasy. If we are concerned about something, about
whether something is beautiful or ugly, fine or wretched,
then we try out that language haltingly, then arguments
and definitions fall out of our hands and we look for images, visionary fragments, shreds of dreams and intuitions,
cries and invocations—you-man, you-god, you-death.

Wherever I go—you!
Wherever I am—you!
Only you and once more you and always you!

You, you, you!
If I am all right—you!
If I am hurt—you!
Only you and once more you and always you!

You, you, you!
Heaven—you; earth—you;
Above—you; below—you;
Wherever I turn, at each end
Only you and once more you and always you!
You, you, you!

This Jewish "Song-you" is in the second language.
Children and prophets, troubadours and mystics speak it
when they want to talk about what they see and experience but cannot prove. The only language which may be,
for a moment, sufficient to say and to know what it is to be
born, how and why it is. Language that you can hear
everywhere, that you can cut out of the newspaper, like
this little conversation between a little boy and his mother.

Child: Do spiders eat flies?
Mother: Yes. They catch them in their webs.
Child: Oh. So in the end there aren't any more flies. Why
have there got to be flies?
Mother: Yes, why? Why are there people?
Child: Oh, I know. The world had to be full, didn't it? And
then someone came who knew. Someone from the Catholics.
Someone called God. And he put a whole lot of people on
the world.
Mother: But where did they come from?
Child: From God of course. From God's believing. Probably
from his tummy or something. Didn't you know? Do you
like it now you know? You'll have to tell grandma, then she'll
know as well.
Mother: How did you know all that?
Child: I often dream about believing and lovely churches and
ugly churches and altar servers and carols and so on.
Mother: I thought that you just came from me.
Child: Yes, but mommies came from God and then daddies
came and then children came from their mommies' tummies.

First there was nothing and then God came and then mommies and the planets. What are you doing? Are you writing it down? That's useful. If there's someone who doesn't know, you can just give him that letter.

Sometimes it can be and has to be as simple, as obscurely direct and as impossibly clear as this—mommies and planets mentioned in the same breath, the womb of the mother and the womb of the universe—low and high, near and yet far, God and man so innocently and dreamingly coupled together. The second language brings children and adults together and is equivocal, ambiguous, paradoxical—everything is nothing, here is far away, my son was dead and has now come to life again (as a man said when he got his lost son back). We are one, says a man to a man. Anyone who begins to calculate and count, counts four hands and two mouths, fortunately. But—we are one. Only these words can approximate to the irrepressible and illogical truth of a man and a man.

My most sober calculations
were thrown into confusion, figures
blew from the paper, words
folded up, ideas
swelled and hissing became flat
when I saw and heard you
I passed out

Remco Campert said in his collection of poems, *Dit gebeurde overal* (*It Happened Everywhere*).

Not a code of concepts, not a system of numbers, but a language of images, of likenesses. A word is a seed and the grain of wheat is a man. God's breath hovers over the water in the beginning. Someone is an elephant or a goat. What is light and what is clay? People are light and clay, bittersweet. There are words of bread and there is a body of bread; we are many, yet we are one body. "Just read—things are not as they are." What is there in this fragment by Gerrit Kouwenaar about man?

brother sister
my equal
my dear protoplasm of stone
my food-tray
my gleaming singing birdcage
my heart room
my heavenly colored earthly aviary
my body
individual like me
indivisible likeness super-
ficial wonder drink-
able mirror oh
my content.

Language given across boundaries and always digging into what cannot be said, into that infinitely double ground of reality, language which leaves veiled and concealed what has to remain veiled and concealed, which evokes the paradoxical and the inaccessible of man's existence and makes it present in paradoxical words and images—"my dear protoplasm of stone."

Secret language, in which you live as you live with another person, by approximation, near enough to touch, knowing and not knowing, safe and unsafe. A language which does not force itself on you, but does speak with authority and which appeals to anyone's creative understanding. The only language which is really daring enough for people.

It is not a language of having and understanding, but a language of groping and naming. Not a language of figures and practical utility, but a language of playing and super-fluity, of finger painting and free association.

Not a language that is simply to be seen—a written language, printed letters, isolation. But a spoken language, a language that is heard and understood, opening and binding. Not the language of absolute rulers and totalitarian systems with their censorship and trials of writers, but the language of protest and freedom—Theodorakis against the military régime, Daniel and Siniavski against the Supreme Soviet, Van het Reve against the counsel for the prosecution, Mr. Abspoel and who knows who else—perhaps fifty percent of Dutch Christians. And not the language of a pretentious Church system of thought, with its dogmas and categories and formulas about God and man, salvation, the soul, truth, and the natural law, but the language of preaching and the liturgy, of witness and singing, the birth language of faith.

The second language is the language of myth. What people believe is true and meaningful, what they think is eternal and original, what they see as reality—however terrible this may be—and what they hope is going to happen—all this they express as images in their myths. Not the historically verifiable facts of our existence, but the hidden meaning or the feared absurdity of those facts, our burning inner life—that is what we want to express in the second language.

Did Orpheus ever exist? He is every man who loses his beloved to death. Did Adam ever exist? He is every man who gives names to everything, but is himself empty and barren if another person does not give him an answer. Odysseus and Percival are our own wandering, dreaming souls. In the myth of Orpheus and Eurydice we are made aware emotionally of the intensity of love and separation. In the myth of Cain and Abel we experience the doom of violence. Adam is the myth of man, the vision of our hope. The myth expresses surprise and emotion in images and only the myth is strong and daring enough to express human sorrow.

Every man has his own myths. His own reality—made more beautiful or deprived of its luster—appears to him in the dreams he has during the day or the night, in his fantasies, his stories, and half-expressed words. It is in these too that he assimilates—illuminates or represses—his surprise and emotion.

A little boy of four tells this story to his father. (It appeared later in Simon Carmiggelt's column in a Dutch newspaper).

Once there was a very old flute player.
He had hardly anything to eat.
People didn't throw him bread or anything.
He had hardly anything to sit on or anything,
the old flute player.
He died of hunger.
He had hardly any hair left.
He couldn't play the flute any more.
He was so fat because he was so hungry.
He couldn't eat anything, anything at all.
He hadn't any clothes at all.

The old flute player is a mythical figure. He is man, seen, experienced, lived with, in his wretchedness. He is everyone and he is the little boy himself.

Again and again, we men "think up" mythical figures to embody our passions, our hope, our guilt, our experience of God, our humanity—Prometheus, Sisyphus, David, Elijah, Tristan and Isolde, the good woman of Setzuan,

Balder, and so many others from modern literature, like Lucebert's "air man" and Marten Toonder's people without faces.

The story of their adventures fathoms the depths and expresses the truth of every man's existence. My own individual and chance fate is also expressed in these strange, almost unbelievable figures. Looking in the mirror of these myths, I sometimes recognize myself—in David, crying for his son Absalom, I recognize my father and me, me and my son, before and now, God and his man. In the myths of Israel and Egypt—the ten plagues, the passage through the sea, the bread and the water in the desert—I recognize the eternal and ever-present struggle to be set free from slavery, the fight against the powers of terror and death, man's hoping for a wonder, a miracle. A psalm, an ancient song from Israel, can interpret my misery and throw light on my life.

I can also recognize, in the figure of Jesus of Nazareth as evoked in the gospel, the perspective of my own life— the way I have to go, the person I shall become, the God who is waiting for me. The gospel does not record all the dates and facts of Jesus' life, does not describe what he looked like, how tall he was, whether he had a beard or not, but it does portray his deepest characteristics— what he really was and the man he still is, what remains unimpaired in him by time and death. This son of men is handed down to us like a vision of the future in images and likenesses, in stories of miracles and in revered names. It is said of him that he forgave sins and that he did other and even more impossible things—that he made the blind see, that he wlked on the water, that he washed his friends' feet. Bread and light, the vine, the source of living water, shepherd and lamb, the way and the door—he is called all these in the second language.

"Behold the man," the gospel, the myth of Jesus, says.

All words are worn out and dull, always too great and too empty. Love, peace, you and God and man—in the mouths of men they become simply terms and numbers, again and again. Words betray, mask, and try to lay hands on what cannot be named. They are willful attempts to seize hold of the mystery and kill it by putting it into a well ordered and accurately manipulated vocabulary, attempts to enclose reality within the covers of your own dictionary.

In his collection of verse, *Het gebruik van woorden* (*The Use of Words*), Gerrit Kouwenaar says:

love I write it with such perfect ease
like a finger in flour
honey you say (I think) O
the use of words
means nothing.

The shortcomings of all words are the constant experience of those who live and work in the sphere of the second language. The ultimate cannot be expressed.

Every poem begins hesitatingly, tentatively, approximately, provisionally. Praying, bearing witness, speaking the language of faith, calling people and imagining them is going by fits and starts, becoming less and less certain with every word and preferring to remain silent. But you cannot go on being silent. You have to go on. You have to listen and be heard. It is somewhere between or past words that people find each other and understand each other. "Do not use a torrent of words," the gospel tells us somewhere. And in his *Dichtertje* (*Little Poet*), Nescio says: "Language is poor, desperately poor. Anyone who knows the work of the Fathers knows this."